Many of the poems in this book appeared in the hardback volume of *Faces In The City*. Several new Kavanaugh poems have been added for balance and a few of the longer poems have been edited by the author. *Faces* has always been one of his very favorite books. He wrote it while living in a ghostly old Victorian in San Francisco, wandering its streets and alleys, recording what he saw and felt. He wrote sitting on docks with fishermen and in pubs sipping cold beer. He wrote in crowded parks, on trolley cars and street corners, in churches and hotel lobbies, in coffee shops and restaurants in North Beach, and late at night in the Tenderloin "when the flotsam people crawling from some unrecorded wreck slump in the doorways of deserted stores to warm their legs with the evening news." He looks back on the period as some of the most enjoyable writing he has ever done, and perhaps some of his very best.

The title, *Today I Wondered About Love,* better characterizes what Kavanaugh has to say about loneliness and love. The new book contains the classic and much loved *Ode To A Relationship:* "Well, Marge girl, we've done it all...", the powerfully farsical *Of Women and Men,* and the rhythmic insight into the poet's soul, *I Must Follow Him:*

"I will not walk where pale men walk,
"I will not know their pain,
"I will not honor God or man to live my life in vain."

Here, too, he writes poignantly of the search for love: "Your body brings back childhood smells", or "I met this really attractive girl like the floating one in the shampoo add...", and the touching *Apartment Four Upstairs:*

"Today I wondered about love and saw an old couple
    returning from the market,
"She with her varicose legs...He with his swollen,
    arthritic knee and emphysema wheeze.
"They paused at the bottom of shaky white steps and
    grinned when he handed her the grocery bag.
"She went first, painfully, slowly, he followed,
    stiff hands pushing her rump.
"And at the top he gently goosed her.

"She shrieked a bit, he coughed, they laughed,
    and disappeared inside Apartment Four upstairs."

Here, also, is the brilliantly theatrical: *"It's Friday Night in the City. . . Monday will never come tonight!"*, the romantic "I've never worn clothes as soft as your breasts", and one of his own all time favorites,

"Come walk the city in the late night's silence,
"When the bars have closed and the laughing conventioneer
"Surrenders to the pain lines in his cheeks. . ."

There is new and unpublished poetry: his special birthday poem to a friend which ends, "Today I read your horoscope. . . you're going to meet a very attractive black bear!" Or his unique reflections on flying: ". . . I have this weird impression that a Greyhound bus has sprouted wings, And Amtrak has finally found a way to be airborne and solvent."

Today I Wondered About Love is vintage James Kavanaugh at his best. The humor, the sensitive insight, the love and hope, the freedom and joy, the tears and struggle - the personal work of a very human man that millions have grown to love and to await enthusiastically each new book of his private, universal diary. They will not be disappointed.

Someone asked James Kavanaugh to whom it is that he addresses his poetry. "I write to myself," he said, "and somehow, the words touch the minds and hearts of the men and women like me, "Who dare to ask of life everything good and beautiful."

Today I Wondered About Love

JAMES KAVANAUGH

Photographs by
Michael Steinberg

STEVEN J. NASH PUBLISHING
P.O. Box 2115
Highland Park, Illinois 60035
Phone: 1-800-843-8545

TODAY I WONDERED ABOUT LOVE

For information address:
STEVEN J. NASH PUBLISHING
P.O. BOX 2115
HIGHLAND PARK, IL 60035

Large portions of this book were previously published under titles of:
Faces In The City and *Will You Still Love Me.*

Previous Printings:
  Nash Publishing of Los Angeles: 9 editions from 1972-1975.
  Harper and Row of San Francisco: 3 editions from1985-1988.

Library of Congress Card Catalogue number:
ISBN #1-878995-07-3

Printings:	25	24	23	22	21	20	19	18	17	16	15	14	13

Thirteenth Printing

First Steven J. Nash Edition
Printed in USA

OTHER BOOKS BY JAMES KAVANAUGH

NON-FICTION:
There's Two Of You
Man In Search of God
Journal of Renewal
A Modern Priest Looks At His Outdated Church
The Struggle Of the Unbeliever (Limited Edition)
The Birth of God
Between Man And Woman (co-authored)
Search: A Guide For Those Who Dare Ask Of Life Everything Good
 and Beautiful

POETRY:
There Are Men Too Gentle To Live Among Wolves
Will You Be My Friend?
Faces In The City
America: A Ballad
The Crooked Angel (children's book)
Sunshine Days and Foggy Nights
Maybe If I Loved You More
Winter Has Lasted Too Long
Walk Easy On the Earth
Laughing Down Lonely Canyons
Today I Wondered About Love
 (Adaptation of: Will You Still Love Me?)
From Loneliness To Love
Tears And Laughter Of A Man's Soul

FICTION:
A Coward For Them All
The Celibates

ALLEGORY:
Celebrate the Sun: A Love Story
A Fable: The Story Of Love and Greed

To those

    Who have struggled from greyness to laughter,

    Who have not given up despite fear and demons

    Who still believe in the healing power of love.

And gratefully to you

    Who have loved me in my madness.

Today I Wondered About Love

INTRODUCTION

I have often envied people who seem to walk through life without obvious love wounds or major marital disasters. They seldom appear deeply depressed, rarely talk of failure or tragedy, and live without intense grief or explosive anger. Apparently they enjoy a secret revelation from birth that was denied the rest of us in our experience of painful love detours and head-on spousal collisions. The charmed ones find love easily and live contentedly while many of us often wonder if true love really exists.

If I'm really honest, I've been confused about love for years, despite the facile definitions of ancient philosophers and modern columnists. Although I've used the word as freely as the smiling and unscarred, what many of us call "love" is often only guilt. Despite self improvement campaigns, we struggle with our abundance of "shoulds." Guilt often infects our relationship with parents well into adulthood. It invades marriages and intrudes on friendships. It has turned many of my Christmases into commercial madness.

I haven't always recognized my guilt as dishonest and destructive. Since our whole culture reeks of guilt, it is hard to tell the truth, even to ourselves. Many of us go to church long after we find it not only pointless but painful. We maintain friendships with people we don't even like, and we frequently marry or stay married only out of guilt. We may smile when we want to scream and punish ourselves when we deserve a medal. Many of us learn to be experts at guilt, veritable honor students of parents and teachers who majored in guilt from infancy.

Guilt aside, "love" to me usually meant the relationship between man and woman. It meant finding a perfect woman to replace my mother and meet my expanding list of needs. No matter how exhausting the pursuit, I would keep looking until I found her. If one marriage didn't work, another would. Thus I spent my energy looking before, after, during and between my two marriages—looking at just about anyone but myself. On the advice of a prominent lady "seminar," I once made a list of the forty qualities I wanted in a fantasy mate. Or was it fifty? I was told that if I truly *believed,* my perfect mate might well call me that very day. Only mother called, asking if I'd forgotten her phone number.

Finally, weary from my search, and still envying those who danced through life, I had to face my loneliness and gnawing private needs or fall apart. I began to recognize the hurt and angry child within me, who still pleaded for the perfect love he never had. And never would, unless he found it within himself. It took a messy divorce to learn that what wounded women called "love" was life-long security and a perfect daddy. It was harder to admit that what I called "love" was lust for every appealing woman I met: to heal me with her sumptuous sex, eternal beauty, and perfect mothering.

This painful awareness slowly expanded my understanding of love beyond sex and guilt. I had heard a thousand times that I must first learn to love myself, but nobody ever told me how. I continued to believe that self love grew from accomplishments, male bravado, and the total love of a miraculous woman. It hurt to admit that I was a facade behind which lived a still frightened boy whom neither sex nor success made whole. Psychotherapy helped me to understand myself, but finally did not rescue me. Friendly churches gave me comraderie and further insights, but religious rituals seemed as helpless as psychology to erase a lifelong wound, or to offer me a customized answer about love.

Finally I was able to accept my confusion, and try to forgive my private and public bungling of love relationships. For years I'd blamed the people who played a significant part in my personal development. When that didn't help, I blamed myself, believing I must be uniquely wounded, since love and happiness eluded me despite sincere effort. At times of great pain, I blamed even God. Only after wandering the side streets of my mind and of number-less cities here and abroad, did I observe that most everyone I met was as confused and crippled as I was. Then I was finally able to wonder about love. And even to laugh.

This book is a diary of my private reflections about love as I wan-dered through New York and Los Angeles, Chicago and San Fran-cisco. It is a journal of wonder and laughter at the madness and mystery of the men and women of every age I studied in their in-tense pursuit of love. Or their tragic denial of its very existence. Assuredly there's nothing humorous about human suffering, but I know that laughter can offer balance and healing for love's deep-est wounds. Even now the endless saga of human love continues to explode everywhere amid pain and despair, forgiveness and fear, hope and laughter. And thus, as always, whether gently observ-ing you and your children, or listening to the private whispering of my own heart, TODAY I WONDERED ABOUT LOVE.

James Kavanaugh
Chicago

IN THE MELANCHOLY
OF SOFT RAIN...

WHO WILL LOVE ME
IN MY MADNESS?

Who will love me in my madness
  When the fearsome mornings come without warning
  In the melancholy of soft rain
  And the dull grey days?
  When I dare not tell you who I am
  Patched together with string
  Fumbling, fearful, lost?

Who will love me in my madness
  When you seek to lean on me
  To glean from me some strength
  That yesterday I seemed to have?
  When I'm sure that I have failed
  And am not strong at all
  And want to run away?

Soon my madness will be gone
  And I will laugh every time I see the sun
But in those mad and fearful times
  Who will love me?

OF SOFT CLOTHES

I've never worn clothes
   As soft as your breasts
Nor slept on silken sheets
   As gentle as your face.
Maybe if you went away
   I'd care about clothes or sheets
Or the rugs on the floor
   And wonder how I can live
Without a garbage disposal
   On this busy street with whining wheels
And sirens all night long.

But now I know that
   Joy is where you are
Peace where you live.
   No seascape I've ever seen
Can match that look in your eyes.
You bring the islands to me, the palms and the gulls.
   And when I wake
Amid traffic and garbage trucks and screaming sirens
   I smile.

SOME ANGRY MAN
APPEARED LAST NIGHT

Some angry man appeared last night
   Summoned by the genie of gin,
A stranger, vague, but remembered,
Frightening, fierce wounded, wounding.
Who trampled on wisdom and gentleness
   Earned in so many battles won,
   Fashioned by so many wounds
   Discovered and healed.

Today the angry man is gone, and in his wake
   Shattered statues, altars overthrown - and shame.
The grinning genie is appeased,
   He proved his point:
Fury still lurks in silent corners
And gentleness must hesitate to claim a victory.

YOUR BODY

Your body brings back childhood smells
   Fruit jars in a damp cellar
   Bread dough rising near the fire
   The musk of burning leaves
   Tomatoes ripening on the vine
   Cornsilk cut for cigarettes
   Sheets and T-shirts dried in the wind
Your body brings back childhood smells
   Apples turning to cider
   Freshly cut pumpkins
   Mother's winter coat
   Dad's easy chair
   Incense and candles in the old church
   The pantry at grandma's house
   Your body brings back childhood smells
   And friends I've known
   And moments when "someday"
   Promised everything.

I WANT
TO REST

I want to rest in your womb
        And stare in liquid eyes of innocence,
Eyes that have known unbearable pain
        Without losing their lustre,
Eyes that reach out and touch,
        That understand all there is to know
          without a word.
I want to bury myself in your softness,
        To lose my being in your breasts,
To love each moment as if it is my last.
I cannot touch enough like some mistreated child
        Who has finally discovered trust and surrender.
I know tomorrow will come and already its shadows
        rise up to deprive me of this moment,
But I ignore their intrusion and cling softly to you.

HAPPY
BIRTHDAY

I heard that the day you were born:
  A buzzard surprised an eagle in its nest,
  A caterpillar was seen dancing on its tail,
  Two ducks were heard to sing the national anthem,
  Stars were seen in downtown Pittsburgh,
  And the New York cab drivers were briefly silent.
Today I read your horoscope, and learned
  That you're going to meet a very attractive black bear.

YOU'RE NOTHING SPECIAL,
SILLY MAN

You're nothing special, silly man
   Save of your own making.
   A fantasy of someone's aching,
   Someone who needs you
      Because the nights are long,
   Someone too desperate to be alone,
   Someone to figure you out,
And to make of your trembling an orgasm.

It's not your fault, silly man,
You're a god who makes love from clay.
   It all began with mothers' wombs
      Feeding you alone
      Protecting you alone.
   It all began with mothers' hands
      Holding you alone,
      Loving you alone.
But you will know
   In the eyes that wander
   In the hands that pull away,
You will know
   When your arms are betrayed
   And love is gone,
That you're nothing special, silly man.

A LONELY
LADY'S EYES

A lonely lady's eyes looking for love,
Knowing it will never come,
Obvious eyes, longing, hurting,
Too weary for games anymore,
Silent eyes, tired of an empty bed,
No one to touch in the night's stillness,
No odor save her own grown inoffensive,
Not even a shoulder to kiss, or hair to caress.
Who will save her from the afternoon movies?

Even now the eyes grow guarded as I stare,
Afraid of one-night stands,
Sensuality turned mercifully dull,
Hungry, hungry eyes,
Wounded, tender eyes,
Angry, frightened, hopeless eyes,
So many mysteries in a single glance,
So many tears unshed on dark eye sills
With no one left to be wept for.

A SHY
CHILD'S EYES

A shy child's eyes
Look out and say
  "If I come outside,
  "Will you promise not to hurt me?"

The body emerges first
Sliding carefully like a cat
Dragging the eyes behind
  To take the dare
  And dive in cold water
  Or lace up skates with frozen hands
  Or swim across the channel
To please the people who are not respecters of eyes
  Until one day the eyes appear at little slots
  From behind rusty, iron walls
  And look carefully out
  Begging not to be hurt.

I HAVE A FRIEND
WHO NEVER LAUGHS

I have a friend who never laughs,
   A strange and silent man
   Who speaks to only a few -
      And rarely.
   He follows the fog
   Stands on high hills
   Drifts along the ocean
   Walks among rocks
   And disappears in eerie caves.
Or he wanders along the river
   Where the cold air
   Makes the children shiver.
And when I asked him why he never laughs
He said that nothing was very funny anymore.

FAMILIES
TO BE FOUND

In the city
   There are families to be found
   Scattered lavishly around
   In silent places
      To replace the one that's lost
         By death
         Or distance
         Or quarrels never healed
            As happens.

There is a grandmother for those who need one,
      Grey-haired and gentle
      With cakes to bake
      And love left over - never used.
There is a grandfather for those who want one
      Quiet and eccentric
      With gifts to buy
      And stories left over - never used.

In the city
   There is blood-love
      The kind that flows
         When hearts expand.
   There is cross-breeding
      And genealogies are mended
         Or improved.
   There are families to be found.

A STONE

Once a little stone
  Was lying in a field
Till someone picked him up
  Polished him
Joined him with other stones
  And made him part of a wall.
He wasn't a stone anymore
  Free to lie in the dust
Until the rain came
  To make him clean again.
He was cemented in a wall
  Surrounded, crowded by other stones.
He was hardly noticed before
  Now everyone saw the wall
Of which he was a part.
  But the wall was in a field
And did nothing, protected nothing
  Led to nothing.
It was only a wall in a field
  Standing alone made by men
Who thought they should use the stone for something.
  And the little stone will remain there
Till the wall falls down
  Or someone knocks it down.
Then he will be a stone again
  And get dusty, feel the rain
And the soft feet of children.

IT'S SUNDAY,
I'VE READ THE PAPERS

It's Sunday, I've read the papers and I leave my room
   In the city in search of the neighbors I once knew,
Looking for someone to call me my
      Special childhood name.
I like the streets, the curio shops and quiet antiques,
   Bars and restaurants, sirens hardly heard amid
      snarled traffic and gawking tourists.
A toughness here among the poor, fewer expectations.
But I am a stranger, awkward, afraid, out of touch.
I don't belong. The old ladies do, shuffling along
   with their shopping bags.
The old men do, letting down awnings and opening crates.
Even the young, angry, pushing, glancing, narrow eyes,
      Not yet wise enough to be sad or afraid.

It's Sunday, I've read the papers, I leave my room
   In the city. New York won, Chicago lost. Big deal!
I want to go back to a gentler neighborhood so long ago,
   Where every house and dog and child had a name.
Hamburgers after football, no claim check at the cleaners.
   Milk bottles on the porch, hole in the screen door.
Choose teams in the park, tease the girls I want to touch,
   Laugh and find familiar cracks in sidewalks.
Instead I hear the accents I do not understand and wonder
Why the slave is gentler than his master
      And more at peace.
   I'll empty the crate, I'll let the awning down,
Take my chains, I've paid dearly enough, smile at me,
      Please smile at me!

It's Sunday, I've read the papers, and I leave my room
   In the city to find a little boy I once knew, to drift
And dream, stumble over curbs, to hide in climbing trees
   And wait for pot roast and gravy and lemon pie.
Instead I hide in the coffee house and watch the radical
   Mark his books with yellow crayon,
         Talking ponderously of
Society and man, blind to the sun making jeweled pat-
terns
   On the faces of the poor. Weaned too soon like me, else
He might have played a flute, caressed a child, or smiled.
Give him a laughing girl whose breasts
      Bounce as she runs,
   Too joyful to know what he's talking about, or care,
And Nietzsche and Marx will lose out to flower picking,
      Squirrel watching and rolling in the grass.

It's Sunday, I've read the papers, and I leave my room
   In the city to wander the woods with my dog, Sandy,
Or to steal a chocolate caramel from the grocer's bin,
   To wave at the bus driver who knows my dad,
And to find the policeman who used to muss my hair.
Instead I'm back on the streets, lonely, empty, alone.
   I think I must go home. But where's home?
Certainly not amid multiple options
      And money in the bank.
I must return to the neighborhoods where I belong.
   My clothes don't show it, nor my face, only my gut.
Mother, hold me, I'm your boy. It's Sunday!
   Mother, hold me, I've read the paper -
      Even the funnies!

TO WALK

To walk when you fear to keep going,
To stand when you long to lie down,
To believe when there's no way of knowing,
To seek when there's naught to be found.
To live with regrets without bending,
To love without hope of return,
To begin when you don't know the ending,
To give a hundred times more than you earn.
To smile when you doubt about living,
To laugh when you'd like to despair,
To forgive when you're filled with misgiving,
To survive when none seems to care.
To try when success is a stranger,
To persist when strength disappears,
To confront the threatening dangers,
To challenge a lifetime of fears.
To look till you find what you're after,
To search earth and the vastness above,
To trust in the power of laughter,
And the final victory of love.

PORTRAITS...

APARTMENT
FOUR UPSTAIRS

Today I wondered about love
  And saw an old couple returning from the market,
  She with her varicose legs
    Like splotches of grape jelly on bread,
  He with his swollen, arthritic knee
    And emphysema wheeze.
They paused at the bottom of shaky, white steps
And grinned when he handed her the grocery bag.
  She went first, painfully, slowly,
  He followed, stiff hands pushing her rump.
And at the top he gently goosed her.
  She shrieked a bit, he coughed,
They laughed and disappeared inside apartment four up-
stairs.

I SAW
HIS FACE

I saw his face today
   More handsome than most
   Formed in an Arab village
   Laughing in the sweet air of Lebanon.
   Chasing goats in the rocks of Syria
   Or shouting in the muddy water holes of Jordan.
I saw his face on the subway
   Profile of a diplomat
   Black hair stiff as richo's palms
   Nose strong as Mount Nebo
   Jaw firm as ancient cedars
   A sullen wisdom about the brow
   Face of a nomadic king, a bedouin seer,
   Patient enough to govern and to understand.
But then I saw his eyes
   Beaten soft and silent into subjection
   A docile camel's eyes that once had lived
   Made submissive and afraid in bondage
   And I wanted to ask
   "How did it happen, my friend?"

A FUNNY
LITTLE SMILE

He's got a round, puffy face
  With sad, red-rimmed eyes behind tinted glasses
  His mouth set in a funny little smile
  And he smacks his lips when he sips his martini.
He's an executive and he drives a big car
  And waits for his wife just as long as she wants
  Because he's grown old enough to compromise
  And to know that happiness
  Comes only now and then.
So he's got a round, puffy face,
  With sad, red-rimmed eyes behind tinted glasses
  And his mouth is set in a funny little smile.

OF ALL
THE PROFESSIONS

Of all the professions that are devious and dirty,
Let's say there are perhaps twenty-five or thirty,
I would say that lawyers somehow lead the list
Of professionals who really get me pissed.
The union plumbers often have a greedy way about them
And real estate developers will often double deal;
Car salesmen are thought to be duplicitous and cunning
But lawyers learn to steal.

I've been cheated by mechanics grinding more than valves
And I've learned that doctors practice usury and medicine;
I've been ill advised by brokers
     Who can't advise themselves
And I wish electricians had to take an oath to Edison.
Morticians make additions in the cost of man's demise,
Police and politicians have been known to take a deal,
The labor union tactics seldom come as a surprise
But lawyers learn to steal.

Thus our system leaves its victims in the cold
Whether wife or husband, worker or employer
Because anyone who's wronged is quickly told
"You'd better get a lawyer."

LITTLE BOY

Little boy lost in color and sound
Sucking in the visions of the town
  Laughing on cable cars
  Wandering through crowded stores
Free to see
  To hear
  To be,
Oblivious even to me.
Absorbed enough to stumble,
  To spill his coke
  To forget where he is
  To forget who he is
Too busy to brush his hair.
Too alive to wash his face
Too much himself to talk until he feels like it.
Knowing what he wants and asking for it
Wandering among ten thousand
  Who do not know what they want
  And if they did
  Would be afraid to ask.

SOMEHOW

Somehow his friends didn't know it
  Though commuting together each day,
Somehow his face didn't show it
  - The incredible price that he paid.

Promptly he traveled each morning
  After jogging and kissing his wife.
How did it come without warning
  - This pitiable snuffing of life?

Here was a man of the city
  In the prime of production and speed,
Not a pale one to mother and pity,
  - The commuter's commuter, indeed.

Would I could finish the story
  With a bold, cinematic-like flair.
Somehow the end should be gory
  - That he died in a duel in the square.

Would he had challenged commuters
  Or had leaped from the twenty-third floor,
Would he had smashed the computers
  Or left with a great, final roar.

What in his life had unmasked him
  That he lay down his head and just died?
Why when the operator asked him:
  "Please dial nine for outside!"?

THE CITY
IS MAN'S MADNESS

The city is man's madness,
  A tower of Babel to defy the gods of time and death,
  A woman sneaking glances in store windows
  Wondering about sagging breasts
      and wrinkles in her neck,
  A man pulling in his stomach, brushing hair
      over his baldness,
  The young laughing and crying without having to try,
  The old living and dying without knowing why,
  People scurrying, running, hurrying,
  People desperate, anxious, worrying.
      People mounted in clusters.
The city is man's madness
  A perverted seed of Adam spilled at the head of rivers,
  A dream fashioned by the side of man hidden
      in shadows,
  The master plan of a sadist never satisfied
      Who tears down buildings to build bigger ones,
  Tragedy time, when brothers hate brothers
      To cling to their jobs,
  A giant colony of cannibal ants
          rushing in all directions
  Because the word is out a beetle died.
So man has built his cities
  Raised the price of land till each building
      Leans on every other,
  Built until the sky is beyond reach or recognition

And in every building, screened from the stars,
  There's a king, faceless and nameless,
And in every office too
  A king
In every crevice as well
  A king fighting for his kingdom,
    Battling like a beast for a piece of ground
      Big enough to be buried on.

THE POLICEMAN
CAUGHT ME TODAY

The policeman caught me today
　　With his big, red, rotating light
When I picked up hitchhikers too far from the curb,
　　A boy with a yellow beard, a stringy-haired girl
　　And two very happy dogs.
The policeman lectured me today
　　With his big, red, rotating face
Pivoting angrily on his big, red, rotating neck.
　　I wanted to laugh - since he seemed overdressed
With a big, fat gun in his belt,
　　A sawed-off shotgun on his dashboard,
And a club as big as a Little League baseball bat
　　Facing a gentle boy and girl and two very happy dogs.

The policeman gave me a ticket today
　　Because I endangered lives,
Though the streets were quiet, the traffic thin
　　And the sun brighter than the big, red, rotating light.
Then he was off with justice satisfied,
　　　secret scars avenged,
　　To rummage through backpacks, to apprehend speeders
With the same red, rotating face
　　That captured murderers and rapists.
The car was quiet, the happy dogs growled,
　　And it made me wonder
What kind of kids
　　Would grow up and want to be policemen.

I MUST
FOLLOW HIM

Some Gaelic sailor lost at sea
   Still lives inside my limbs.
From time to time he calls to me
   And I must follow him.
I wander from the city's lights
   To walk along the bay,
I hear the creaking, restless ships
   That draw me far away.
I drink my beer in brawling bars
   And scorn the life I lead,
I pause at night to hear the sound
   Of foghorn symphony:
The snorting tubas in the haze,
   The groaning of trombones,
The oboes, flutes, the violins,
   The moaning baritones.
I sleep with lusty women
   Who taste of salt and sand
Whose arms are like the groaning waves
   And legs are like the, land.
My beard grows free as winter squalls,
   My skin like canvas-sails,
I have no time for scholars' words
   But only seamens' tales.

I feel the night upon my face,
   The sun upon my skin,
I taste the salt upon my lips.
   My heart beats hard within,
My hands grow tough, my body lean,
   I take no note of time,

I sleep in clothes I've worn all day
   And smell of sweat and grime.
And I swear that I will not return
   To pallid, somber men
Or lie on sallow-women's sheets
   Or lose my life again.
I will not live by rules of fools
   Where scoundrels say what's fair,
I will not live in city streets
   Where death is in the air.
I will not walk where pale men walk,
   I will not know their pain,
I will not honor God or man
   To live my life in vain.

And when he leaves, this rugged man,
   And I am all alone
I make my way through city streets
   And climb the stairs to home.
My heart is happy once again,
   My chest is strong and free,
I settle down to live my life
   Until he calls to me.
And someday soon, I know full well,
   When pallor chalks my skin
The Gaelic sailor lost at sea
   Who lives inside my limbs
Will once again call out to me
   And I will follow him.
Will once again call out to me
   And I will follow him.

THE BUILDING
INSPECTOR

It really would be nice to remodel the basement.
  Do it myself - it'll hardly cost a thing.
I'll have a pool table, a party room, murals,
  Maybe a sauna bath and a real wine cellar.
Not that I drink a lot of wine, but it's nice to say
  "And here's my wine cellar." That's class.
I'll get my permit, start digging a bit,
  Get the floor in. Nothing to it. I should what?
Reinforce the foundation? It looks okay to me, inspector.
  Well, of course, I want to do it right.
    You only do it once in your life.

I need a new storm drain, concrete below the mud sill?
  What's a mud sill? And a two-inch vent?
The furnace pipe is too low? Too old?
  Dig four inches deeper? But it's just a party room.
Well, it would be inconsiderate of my seven-foot friends.
  Another window? And a fire exit? Of course, inspector.
I want it right. You only do it once in your life.
  Hello, inspector? You can't come till Friday?
But the ready-mix man is here, he charges by the minute
  And the countdown's begun.
    Could you talk to the plumber
Who's talking to the carpenter
  While waiting for the gas man?
It really would be nice to remodel the basement.
  Do it myself - it'll hardly cost a thing.
You're damn right
  You only do it once in your life.

A QUIET GIRL

A girl waiting for a bus
  On a grey, cold morning,
    The sun still tucked behind buildings,
  Eyes hazy and soft as the air,
  Damp and only half-emerged from sleep,
    Innocent as animal's, as quietly protesting,
The smell of a quilt still on her legs,
  Soft dreams of night still moistening her loins,
  Her coat pulled tight, the wind blowing her hair,
She is silent, almost sullen,
  More beautiful than the night before.
A quiet girl whose face does not frighten me,
A gallant girl, whose body aches a bit,
  Pleading for a little more time in bed
And the bus will come and she will be gone.

POLITICIAN TIME

It's politician time in the city
And candidates gather in old bingo halls,
   Church basements, or dreary lodges
To tell the people of garbage and jails,
   Clean water and no more cavities,
   Sewage tax and buses, ecology and new schools,
   Police chasing prostitutes, police walking streets,
   Drug traffic, game rooms for the old, homes for the poor,
And everything for the children.

It's politician time in the city
And restless people gather on folding chairs,
To see old councilmen telling jokes, beat the system,
   Twenty years late, they tore my posters down,
   Stand on my record, sit on my ass.
   Young commissioners, smooth and not Jewish anymore,
   Only pogroms in the blood, Irishmen with bushy hair,
   Good talkers, natural politicians, nice teeth,
   Young idealists, old syndicates, labor tells the story,
   Blacks and browns turning white from martinis and
   handshakes,
   I'm from the people, I walk the streets, I know the people.
     Who knows the people? What people?
Candidate night, paper on tables, paper on the floor,
   Pictures, placards, programs, words,
And everything for the children.

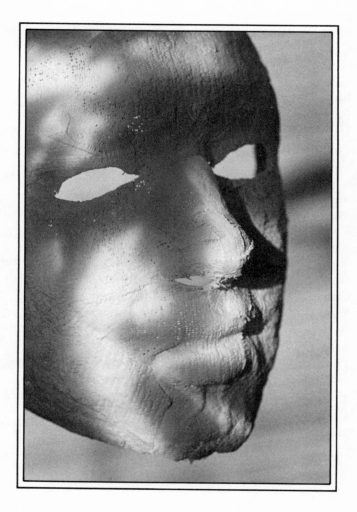

THE MAN
AT THE CORNER CLEANERS

The man at the corner cleaners committed suicide today.
Some trembling hand made desperate took his life away
  And left a familiar corpse with a hole in its head.
We knew him well.
  ...Well...we knew him
And talked of politics and children
    Graft and football games
Of schools and rising prices
    Police and business schemes.
  We never talked of death.

The man at the corner cleaners committed suicide today.
Business has never been better, or so my neighbors say,
The stories of those who knew him grow longer every day,
The old are hushed and silent as they pass along that way
  And no one mentions death.

SERENE OLD LADY
OF THE AFTERNOON

Serene old lady of the afternoon
  Shuffling along sidewalks on aching feet,
  Little patches of hair on legs still beautiful,
  Flesh softer now, resting hesitantly
    on well-traveled bones,
  Sagging gently in submission to what
    the years have told you.
  Head bowed a bit as if to shrink from harshness,
  A child's eyes, but wiser, more alive and moist
  In the breeze that blows the city's dust about.
  Grey hair flecked with specks of auburn
  Recalling what was and knowing that it was enough.

Serene old lady of the afternoon
  Pleased with so little now,
  Laughing at TV cartoons, weeping at soap operas,
  Drawn from memories to the theatre of the sidewalks,
  Revived by city sights and children coming
        home from school,
  By store windows and conversations on the corner,
  Gentle rituals of fish to feed,
  Birds to scold and chatter with, plants to tend,
  A houseful of knick-knack history, a little soup to make,
  Some nice, fresh corn, maybe a pork loin, a tiny one,
  To make the kitchen smell like it used to.

Serene old lady of the afternoon
  I see your sisters angry, embittered,
    Whining, complaining,
Distressed at life's ending, resenting their children,
While somehow you have outwitted death by living,
Somehow moved beyond time and tragedy to wonder,
Until all your wrinkles lead to your eyes and disappear
In some soft and mysterious immortality.

FACES
IN THE CITY

In the city there are faces
　　Confident or afraid, wrinkled or yet unformed,
Wise with experience, or bland and empty hiding pain.
　　　　Joyous faces living each moment
　　　　Or desperate faces passing the time.
Beyond the color and forms are the faces,
　　　　sketches yet unfinished, tragedy and triumph
　　　　fighting for mastery.
Faces changing every day or drawn rigid
　　　To remain the same.
Faces proud of power or bruised by defeat,
　　Searching for love or proclaiming its presence,
　　　　Looking for a way out sudden and magic,
　　　　Or content and joyous to be.
In the city, man is the mystery, not God.

It is our own face we see in the city:
　　Prisons to tell of our pain and despair,
　　Hospitals to tell of our concern and indifference,
　　Homes to tell of our hope and defeat.
　　　　The streets are ours and the beggars,
　　　　The slums are ours and the bells,
　　　　The parks are ours and the children.
We are the bus groaning up the hill,
　　Smiles and curses from taxis,
　　Silent women worrying about Christmas,
　　Salesmen with big smiles and sweaty palms.
No face is alien, no face is not ours,
　　Judges only judge themselves.

The city mirrors our face:
    We live there and laugh there and learn to be afraid.
        The poor are trapped there,
        The rich are rewarded there,
        The lonely are lured there,
        And the lovers are loved there.
    We will curse it, despise it, attack it, abandon it,
        But we will always return.
        Because the city is the face of man.
    There is no noise like the city at midday,
    No silence like the city before dawn.
        The oceans soothe us, the mountains heal us,
        But we will live and grow and die in the cities,
    Because the cities are our face.

The city is you, the city is me,
    Our own eyes that stare back
    When we look and sometimes see,
    Our faces in the city.

OF WOMEN AND MEN...

OF WOMEN AND MEN

Women, indeed, have never been paid
The salaries they've long been deserving,
Feminine nerves are unquestionably frayed
By the chauvinist men they've been serving.

Sisters, indeed, have seldom received
The choices and chances of brother,
Feminine hands have but feebly achieved
In the role of a mistress and mother.

Mothers, indeed have submitted their lives
To the dominance fostered by fathers,
Girls in their teens always longed to be wives
Since their options were molded by others.

Man, it is true, went to work and to war
But consider the freedom he's given -
Males bought the house and purchased the car
Leaving shopping and cleaning to women.

Angels are men and God is a male
Even doctors and lawyers most often,
Men are preferred at Harvard and Yale
And are usually first in the coffin.

Men are retired and women are fired
Only rarely can ladies drive taxis,
Women who hope to be easily hired
Are required to be simple and sexy.

Men have it made, we're gross, overpaid,
We deserved to be quartered in sections,
But ladies be kind and please bear in mind
What it takes to sustain an erection.

CITY GIRL

City girl
    Pursuer of fashions, up on plays,
    Frenetic enough, good at words,
    Reader of magazines, critic of movies,
    Tight around the lips,
    Red wine with beef
    And sex after dinner and the late news.
City girl
    What shall we talk about tonight?
    The effect of LSD on babies?
    Murders in the city - and rapes?
    Did you know that a beggar stabbed three men
    On their way from the ice follies?
    You read it, too?
City girl
    I like it when you drop your guard,
    Your eyes go droopy and soft,
    Your breath sounds helpless,
    Your face prepares for some explosion,
    And touching replaces talking.
    Maybe that's why I hurry you to bed.
City girl
    Your window box looks like a garden now,
    Your fish tank bubbles like a waterfall,
    Cars on the street sound like crickets and frogs
    And lonely owls in the night.
    And I can taste the country on your lips.

SIGGY AND BABS

Siggy married Babs
    Because she was poised and sophisticated,
    Could talk about anything at parties,
    Had an MA in French literature
        With minors in Cordon Bleu cooking
        And Eurasian Art,
    And had been in analysis for seven years.

Babs married Siggy
    Because he was a prominent attorney,
    Was successful in the commodity market,
    Could talk about anything at parties,
    Had written a book about the
        Crime rate in Pakistan,
    And had been in analysis for eleven years.

Siggy divorced Babs
    Because she was poised and sophisticated
    And never stopped talking about
        Her MA in French lit, her cooking
        And Eurasian Art,
    And the seven years of analysis.

Babs divorced Siggy
    Because he was a prominent attorney
    And he couldn't shut up about
        His success in commodities,
        The crime rate in Pakistan,
    And the eleven years of analysis.

A year after Babs entered the convent,
Siggy married a high school graduate
    Who didn't know torts from sow bellies
    And presumed Freud was wanted for
        Indecent exposure in Pakistan.
    But she makes great jell-o with raspberries in it,
    Laughs loudly at all his jokes,
    And has long legs that turn him on.
They've been happily married for eleven years
    And have four great kids.

THIS REALLY
ATTRACTIVE GIRL

I met this really attractive girl
　　Like the floating one in the shampoo ad
Who found me as exciting as a sought-after man
　　Like maybe an actor or a DJ with his own show
And she really listened while I talked
　　A hell of a lot more than I intended to.
And after dinner in her favorite restaurant
　　Where she knew the waiters and the "in" wines
And a lot of guys really stared at her
　　Which made me, so to speak, very proud,
We really got it on, after I circled the block four times
　　Trying to find a parking space and to retain my poise.

And all the time I kept thinking about this woman friend
　　Who is no mistress of the manuals
And really no match for this really attractive
　　Shampoo girl
　　But with whom I laugh a lot and talk
　　Only when I want to.
I thought about watching a movie on TV,
　　Eating pizza on the floor, picking my feet
　　and spilling my drink as usual, and hearing
"Do you wanna?" And answering
　　"I dunno, do you wanna?"
　　Until we fell asleep just holding each other.
All of which led me to believe
　　There's a hell of a lot to be said for comfort.

SOUL-MATES

If I found you, what would I do.
    Start laughing, then make love,
    Cook dinner, then take a shower,
    Plant roses and peach trees,
    And buy two gentle horses.
    Find chickens and three pigs
    Build a house and make jam
    Go to New York and see shows
    Go to China and eat shrimp
    Have a baby, then two more.
    Read books and improve our tennis
    See every movie and fix the stereo.
    Get stoned and laugh all night
    Write a book and tell the world!

ODE
TO A RELATIONSHIP

Well, Marge girl, we've done it all
   Remember the yoga sessions - how I
      Straightened out my spine
     Until I stretched my knee ligaments
   And then we went to the sensuality classes
     And you finally had your orgasm,
      Standing up - in line -
While we were waiting to see the porno movies.
   And then the two months of group sex right after
     We took the classes in learning how to fight
   And we separated our apartment from the kids
     And started childlike to eat popcorn in bed
     Like the man from the seminar said.
   And we confronted each other and dealt with things
     Whether we wanted to or not
And we went to the Jesus happening and then
     The guitar Masses
     And I became a block captain in the twelfth precinct.
   Remember how I learned to play the guitar
     And we sought new answers in the stars
   And I dropped out of the scouts and the rotary
     And we got our ten-speed bikes.
   Then we tried massaging each other
     In orange flower water
     And tried 21 new positions until your back gave out.
   Then the trip to Europe, and we learned to make
     Our own pottery, grew marijuana in the basement
     And did that thing on mescaline
     Until the porch swing broke.

Then we moved to the country, Marge,
   Grew our own vegetables
   Took vitamin E, and learned to fly fish.
Then we got the sauna and you began to read cards
   And brought the guru to stay with us for a month
   Until he choked while braiding his hair.
And I gave up cigarettes, girl, then booze
   And we both got hooked on kumquats.
Then the commune summer, the swingers' party
   And the extensions classes
   And we sold our stocks and invested in real estate
   And stopped seeing your mother, and even mine.
Remember, Marge, remember...
   Well now I know what it is, baby.
   It's you, and I'm splitting.
You piss me off!

THERE SEEMS TO BE
EVERY INDICATION

There seems to be every indication,
Given our personal freedoms in this century,
   That a proper book on sex will soon be written.
Not one that simply tells of techniques
   Or hangups, or daring positions,
But one that encompasses the history of sex
   And the discoveries, the breakthroughs
   With proper credit lines.
Thus, for example, what school child realizes that
   The English lathe operator, Isaac Henderson Jones,
   Discovered twelve hundred and seven erogenous zones?
Or who has heard of
   The Frenchman Jean-Paul Curriere Rippe
   Who measured the thrust of a rotating hip?
Or did you yourself know that a black man,
   The immortal South African, Gerard Duncan Speers,
   Was the first to make use of the circular mirrors?
And a little closer to home
   That the American publisher, William Adair,
   Was the very first man to print pubic hair?
And isn't there room for a chapter or two
On the bizarre deviations of charismatic leaders
   Like the great naval hero, Washington Lammock,
   Who could only perform in a zebra-striped hammock?
Barring sexual backlash and sudden underpopulation,
There seems, indeed to be every indication
   That a proper book on sex will soon be written.

YOU WERE DESIGNED

You were designed by wispy angels
    To give the earth gentleness and love,
Sculpted by the warm hands of the centuries
    To give delight to wandering eyes
    And make hearts beat with strange energy.
Your face speaks of ancient lore
    And mysteries yet to be revealed.
Your body flows like the white sand dunes
    of a Michigan lake from childhood.
You were created to walk and talk with,
    To hold and caress on winter nights.
You were filled with love and giving,
    Made to tip-toe across the waves in gossamer
      to touch the moon.
Most of all you were made for me,
    And every least glance tells me with eloquence
How much you love me.

TO GIVE
EACH REALITY

To give each reality its own identity,
    And not mine.
To rejoice in the color of a chair,
    The bloom of a rug, the gentle warmth of a lamp.
To see the compassionate eyes of a dog,
    The curious eyes of a cat,
    The innocent, frightened ones of a rabbit,
And to know that they are their own being.
To see dawn as its own glory and the moon
      as its own splendor,
The day and night as neighbors, possessed of
      their own being beyond any delight of mine.
To see you as fragile and strong, as hungry
      and well nourished,
As your own essence and not a reflection of mine.
To rejoice in you for what you are
    And not for what you bring to me.

Then finally to see myself for what I am
    And not for what others want me to be,
Not even for what my fears and vanity
    Would fashion me to be.
This is to be free, to be totally alive,
    This, above all, is to love!

IT'S FRIDAY NIGHT
IN THE CITY

It's Friday night in the city
  The singles' bars explode to announce the weekend
  For which the week was made.
  Slow down, Monday will never come tonight.
  Find the eyes that look back,
  Start a conversation. Find the words.
  Don't let her drift away. Slow down. It's early.
  Not much of a face, but check the body.
  Rooted, earth mother, something to cling to.
  Find the combination. Make it right.
  Loosen up. Not too heavy. Get another drink.
  Make her laugh - they like to laugh.
  The regulars move easily.
  The frightened talk too much.
  The cabs are spitting out the strangers.
  Big in their own territory.
  It's not too late. Remember that night in Boston?
  Divide and conquer. Which one do you want?
  Touch her arm. Easy, not too fast.
  Move her out. Too noisy to talk. Get some air.
  You're home. It's Friday.
  Monday will never come tonight.

It's Friday night in the city
  The neighborhood bars explode to announce
      the weekend
  For which the week was made.
  Familiar faces. Friendly. Refuge.
  Time for bowling scores and golf swings.
  Time to hear about Harry's divorce.

Dave's got a new story. Tell it again.
Couples laughing, couples talking,
Couples sitting quietly, familiar territory.
Play a game of pool, shake the dice for music.
Buy a drink for the ladies. The usual.
Pockets of people. Someone knows my name.
Al's drunk again. Arguing. Get him a cab.
Tenderness. Understanding. Cut him off.
Funny since he lost his wife.
Where are we? Somewhere. Anywhere.
Kids got the flu. School's too crowded.
Mother died. Sorry to hear it. She wasn't old.
How's the new job? Chance to make some money.
Car broke down again. New baby coming.
Go home. Happy. Laughing. It's Friday.
Monday will never come tonight.

It's Friday night in the city
The streets explode to announce the weekend
For which the week was made
Restaurants crowded. We have your reservation.
Ladies laughing. Waiters rushing.
Nice to see you again.
Another round. We're not in a hurry.
What do you recommend? Lamb's always good here.
Music. Voices. Leave it to Wally. He knows.
French wine's better. House dressing. More butter.
Medium rare. Romaine lettuce. Isn't that Audrey?
Theatres crowded. Get a cab. Row nine. Not bad.
Called a month ago. Dark suits. Capes. Elegant.
Ladies laughing. Ladies talking. Ladies pointing.

Men smiling. Let's get a smoke. Get a program.
Restrooms crowded. Wait in line. Wash your hands.
Tie looks nice. A little paunchy. Getting older.
Let's have a nitecap. Call the sitter.
Kids got the flu. School's too crowded.
Mother died. Sorry to hear it. She wasn't old.
I'll take the check. Write it off.
Go home. Great evening. Laughing. It's Friday.
Monday will never come tonight.

PRETTY GIRL

Pretty girl playing the games you were taught
   Doing what you know you're good at
      Still a little girl and no one knows.
You should have been plainer pretty girl
   Worried about a crooked nose
      Or teeth that wandered.
Glances come too easily your way
   Never missed a party, always had a name,
      Every day to play the pretty girl game.
Never had to let your daddy go
So you're still a little girl -
   And no one knows.

THERE'S
NO REASON

There's no reason for an available male
    To be troubled by modern women:
I took Marjorie out twice
    And now I'm trying to explain why
    I didn't call on Tuesday night.
Virginia has a weekend planned
    And I can't remember her last name.
Mary Ellen has free passes to Disneyland
    For me and her three kids,
And Donna wants me over for lasagna
    When her spaghetti went down
    Like a den of dead sea serpents.
Beatrice is on such a restricted diet
    That we ended up eating on the floor
    Of a health food store.
And Jenny contacts me twice a day
    To play trivia by phone.
Desiree' wants a platonic friendship
    And wears a bikini that would
    Startle the Riviera.
Sue is a career woman and the only time
    I can see her is during her Yoga class
    On Sunday afternoon.

It's finally becoming clear why men get married.

ARE YOU
SATISFIED?

Are you satisfied my love?
  Did I wait long enough
  Shake hard enough
  Or move slow enough?
Did you come? Or will you?
  Shall we try a new position
Or a new partner?

LET GO OF IT ALL

WILL YOU
STILL LOVE ME?

When the day frightens me
  And the fog refuses to melt before the sun,
When the accusers rise within me from the past
  And tell me I have failed
When I feel scarcely valuable enough to live,
  Will you still love me?

When weariness overpowers me
  And I fear I cannot go on,
When there is no joy in my heart,
  And I struggle to laugh and even breathe,
When I'm afraid I have accomplished nothing worthwhile,
  Will you still love me?

When I am caught in the cocoon of past memories
  And encapsulated in marauding anxieties,
When the bruises of the past make me prisoner,
  And all the things I once dared now seem impossible,
When my thoughts race in a thousand, helpless directions,
  Will you still love me?

When I have finally answered the past accusing voices
  And find consistent delight in the present moment,
When I can laugh far into the night
  And am strong and brave in the morning,
When I have found the serene rhythm of my life-force,
  And can walk without clinging and run without bonds,
When I do not seem to need you - even then,
  Will you still love me?

TONIGHT

Tonight I just want someone to cling to for awhile,
   No words, no analysis, no solutions.
Yesterday I really had it together,
Now there is some weariness beyond all words
   So let me hang on
      For a little mothering or fathering
      Or whatever.
Hold me. Please hold me!
   I'm in another one of those alleys - black and musty,
   Socially unacceptable again.
No questions please. Not even names.
   A cat's not enough. I need you. Not because you're you
   But because you're warm and alive
   And I need you
      Not your mind
      Not your experience
      Not your love.
Just your body. Your arms. You
      Is that so bad?

LET GO OF IT ALL

Let go of it all and see where it takes you.
Let the money slide away and the tense young men
　　Who talk of security and conquests.
Let the cars whiz by, the square jaws and too bright eyes.
Stumble and fall and lie prone upon the earth
　　Until you taste the dirt again and make friends
　　　　with the fog.
Toss your plans aboard the first wind heading north
　　And your ambitions on a breeze heading south.
Let it all descend upon you like lava and sunshine
And let the clouds guide you as they will.
There is no mountain high enough to climb
　　　　with final satisfaction,
　　No hole deep enough to dig, no ocean vast enough to
　　cross.
There is only laughter and peace and the present moment,
　　Your breath in unison with the throbbing earth,
　　Your flight as aimless and transient as the birds.
Let it all go and wash you like the rain,
Let it all go and buffet you like the wind,
Let it all go and see where it takes you
　　Until you are one with the earth and all its inhabitants.

I'M SURE

I'm sure the Russians are not noted for honest trials
And even my own petty disloyalties
    Would warrant a few years
On the waste lands east of Moscow.

I'm also sure I'd rather live here than there
If only because I hate long, cold winters
    And too much cabbage makes me belch -
And other unmentionable things.

On the other hand, when I visit the Bank of America,
Or even its pale, incestuous imitations,
    To garner a decent loan,
Why does the computer say "Nyet!"

SOMETIMES
I FEEL

Sometimes I feel I may have succumbed to the city's ways
Because nothing seems to save me from the way I was,
Which, from mounting evidence and unsolicited advice,
   Seems really terrible
Because it appears that everyone expects to live forever
   Either in this world
   Or in the next
   Or, if at all possible, in both.
It's not that I haven't tried the city's cults.
   I attended the Self-Realization Fellowship -
   Which seems to be a sensible amalgam of East and West
   And perhaps North and South -
   Where our leader reminded us that God
      Does not torture us beyond our endurance -
      Whereas I had never imagined
         He would torture us at all
      Unless, of course, this was a subtle reference
      To the sermon which was fifty minutes long,
   But I did hold my offering loosely in my right hand
      As I was told.
Later I discovered that the scientologists accept
   Personal checks and like to be paid in advance
   Like colleges and dance studios since they have
   Developed a program so ethical and integral that even
   Freud and Jesus would presumably be
      On the mailing list.

Even later the evangelists reported for my edification
   That God gave His only begotten Son for my salvation -
   Which only made me wonder how the Son
      Felt about the gift.

And at a very religious school
   A reformed boy told me that Jesus
      was more powerful than LSD
  Which I knew would make the surgeon general
      Very happy,
  And a girl with rather stern eyes insisted that sex
  Was from the devil which I am ashamed to say
  Only made me wonder how devils do it.
And I followed the Hare Krishna parade
  Which promised to calm my mind for the rest of my life
Whereas the Mormon missionaries
     Wanted me for two years
  Offering me a break on my hospitalization
  And two good acres in Utah.
All of which made me feel terribly guilty
When I gave up my quest and went home
  And watched a very old movie on TV
  And wondered if the stray cat I was feeding regularly
  Really gave a damn about me.

THE FRIENDLY
SKIES

I love the airplane ads
With their talk of smiles
  and friendly skies
Leg room and gourmet food,
Lovely stewardesses and stewards
  Attending my every wish.
There is no mention of disembarking
  At Gate H-37
Which is four miles from the
  ticket counter
When I carry my bags
  because I lost two in
Hartford and waited a
  week for one in Boston.
Of course, nobody's perfect,
  Especially the dancer who
Talks non-stop from Laguardia
  To Los Angeles
And the difficult choice between Manicotti
  And frozen cod with mushrooms,
Which both taste the same
  Even in first class -
I have strange memories
  When flying was fun,
Now I have this weird impression
  That a Greyhound bus has
    sprouted wings
Or AMTRAK has finally found
  A way to be airborne and solvent.

AT
THIS MOMENT

At this moment
  I am all alone.
No heart knows what my heart feels
No lips capture what my lips long to say
No eyes read the message of my face
No ears reassure me that I have been heard.

What do I want you to say?
  Some magic word of love
  To take my sadness away?
I asked too much
  Something no one can give.
Perhaps it is enough to know you care.
  Perhaps enough.

THEY'RE
AFTER ME AGAIN

They're after me again!
It all started when I bought a house
And the insurance companies found out about it
Because my mortgages were suddenly public knowledge
And letters came from all over to tell me that for a fee
They would bet I'd die before the mortgages were paid
And if so they'd appear and leave my house
      all free and clear.

When I refused to bet my house against my life
The insurance companies gave up on me -
Which kind of hurt - and sold my name
To extension classes and correspondence institutions.
I only had to check a single box and I'd get information
On how to be almost anything. Like this one guy
Who had been a part-time gardener
      and ended up a stockbroker -
Which is supposed to be a good deal.

Anyway I considered being a lawyer -
      to fix my own tickets,
Or a CPA - to do my own income tax,
Or I could learn to manage a restaurant
      and meet lonely women,
Or a hotel and get special rooms for my friends.
I could even be a commercial artist
      and paint murals in my bathroom
Or a traffic manager and figure out a better way
      to get downtown
Or I could be a diesel mechanic and take people
      on my own train
To football homecomings, or maybe fill the cars with kids

Who'd never left the city and make enough money
        doing this
To call the insurance companies
        and bet my life against the house.
But with all my dreams I lost the reply card about the time
The scientologists got my address,
        followed by three missionaries,
Two bishops from the Southwest, four pool salesmen
    And a prepaid burial program.
Then apparently the extionsion's classes gave my name
To the book and magazine people since it was obvious that
Without a decent job I had a lot of time to read.

Actually I ended up beating these bastards
        at their own game
Although I finally subscribed to four magazines
        and three book clubs
And an encyclopedia on sex which came almost
        free with the one
        which gave me ten chances on a grand prize
        To pay off the whole damn mortgage!

I CAME
TO THE CITY

I came to the city because man is mostly here
   And will always be - and presently,
     I choose to be where he is.
Once I thought that beauty was only in the mountains,
   Or by the sea, or where forests shelter the flowers.
But I find beauty here as well, confusion grown friendly,
   Discord turned to melody, swarming bodies
     To take attention from my own.
I find beauty when hamsters in pet store windows
   Surprise me like giraffes in a jungle clearing,
   City lights shine from high hills like stars,
   Children wait for buses and still read about Cinderella,
   Lovers laugh and tease in parks and seem as carefree
     And joyful as those by the sea.

Somehow the city is more man than the rest:
   Man is not as overpowering as the ocean,
   Not as serene and distant as the mountains,
   Not as solemn and silent as the forests - only sometimes.
Somehow the city is man:
   Afraid and dauntless, gentle and frenetic,
   Hurting and hoping, living and dying,
   Huddled together and drifting apart,
   Leaping from bridges and skipping from school,
     Afraid, so afraid, but laughing, often laughing.

Reality is on the faces of the people:
    Waiting solemnly for buses, patiently in supermarkets,
    Shyly in clinics, expectantly at movies,
       Despairingly in unemployment offices.
Believing it has to be this way, almost accepting it,
       And laughing, often laughing.
Reality is on the faces of the people
    Finding peace amid traffic, joy amid fear,
    Flowers on a window sill, fresh bread
       And silent gardens,
       Finding a lover from a thousand faces.

Man is here, all sides revealed:
    Here are the people, the horns, the shuffling feet,
    The cabs, the lights, the business beat,
    The shouts, the rush, the crowded streets.
I need you now! I've found you now! Death be still!
       My city lives!

COME,
WALK THE CITY

Come, walk the city in the late night's silence
   When the bars have closed
      and the laughing conventioneer,
   Stripped to his shorts, surrenders to the pain lines
      in his cheeks and wonders if his wife can turn him on,
   When virgins are all safely bolted in bed
   Reading novels to discover how life should be lived,
   When the prostitutes gather to talk of health foods
   And the wealthy regular they knew in Florida,
   When the garbage man begins his day in
      strident disdain
   To gather landfill for future development,
   When the morning papers are bounced from trucks
   Like trussed bodies with a secret story to tell,
   When the city like some aging, weary giant
   Collapses on the pavement to decay and die,
   When the taxis play tag with their golden lights
      in the night
   and deliver drunks who can't find their cars,
   When the flotsam people crawling from some
      unrecorded wreck
   Slump in the doorways of deserted stores
   To warm their legs with the evening news,
   When a misty rain falls upon the mystery men
Who shield themselves in the shadows of the night.

Come, walk the city in the late night's silence
   When the buses are heaped together to rest
      their groaning gears
   And the patrolling police surprise the lovers
      in their cars

When the poor relieve themselves in alleys,
And leave the trees and bushes to the dogs,
When the forgotten men with no more dreams
Wander in their grey garb blending with the night,
When the street lights turn their whiskers
      to golden stubbles of wheat
And transform the haze of their eyes into wistful shine,
When their tattered clothes give them freedom to drift
Into places where policemen carry guns,
And gentle faces made soft and distant by pain too deep
For memory stare at ladies and know that their glances
Will never be returned or will be shuddered at,
When the men free enough to lose their respectability
Approach a stranger for a cigarette or beg for a quarter,
When the men who know they'll always lose
      Quit before the struggle begins
And gather soberly to watch the night get cold.

Come, walk the city in the late night's silence
      To meet the men with no one to count on,
      No one eager for a call, no one to contact on holidays,
      No one to love them at all,
      Meet the fathers and brothers now unclaimed who tell
      Stories of the past and study the eyes of the listener
      To see how long the interest lasts.
      At night the city is more theirs than anyone's,
      It's very curbs their couch, its parks their playground.
      They know the secret corners where the morning sun
      Sneaks through to warm their hands,
            the secluded spots,
      To sleep and fantasize and drink cheap wine
            in paper sacks.

They know the cracks in sidewalks, holes in streets,
The outlines of the buildings, the reflections
   of the moon.
They can spot a tourist, a detective, a pusher, the moods
And temperament of the police. They hear the sirens
And see the crimes, they stand back from life
   as spectators,
Unconcerned with wars or investments
   or rising crime rates.
And when the morning comes and traffic roars
And the successful men and women pour from buses,
File along streets, rush to fill offices and skyscrapers,
They stand along the curbs and watch and wonder,
   and know
That in the night, when the city is silent,
The meek and lonely vagrants take possession
     of the earth.

DOOM
PROPHETS SAY

Doom prophets say
Greedy man will take my world away -
My flowers
My birds
Streams I've fished in
My trees
My ocean
Fields I've wished in.

Doom prophets say
Greedy man will take my life away -
My air
My food
The city sounds and sights
My fog
My bridges
The building shapes at night.

Doom prophets say
That all will pass away.
But I want them to know,
Despite statistics
I don't die easily.

I'M NOT
SURE

I'm not sure that anyone would understand
  In Scottsdale or Winona,
But there are many days
  When the city is so much mine
That the sounds of traffic
  Are the background stereo which soothes me,
When garbage cans piled in alleys
  And lunch bags littered along the curb
Seem like lovers' clothes, recovered in the morning
  Somewhere between the sofa and the TV.

MAN DOES NOT LIVE
IN THE GIANT CITY

Man does not live in the giant city
   But in a town of his own making
      With narrow boundaries
   To shelter him against the enclosing time,
   In a corner somewhere, or a kitchen
   Where someone cares enough to be peevish,
   In a nesting place with a supermarket where
     He can cash checks
   And knows the checkout lady by name,
   A special parking place, bakery smells
      And someone to nod to.
   Familiar faces like halloween masks,
   Assorted friends to keep away the darkness,
   In a town where old men can smell
      The tar of street repair
   And watch the workmen smooth the new cement
   Or see the children skipping home from school
   And making wings and hoods with their coats.

Man does not live in the giant city
   But in a name like New York
   Where he's never seen a play
   But subways in silence till he finds
   The corner where a dog barks at him in recognition.
   He is not as free as his San Francisco
   Nor as energetic as his Chicago
     As pragmatic as his Detroit or Pittsburgh
     Liberated as his Los Angeles
     As elegant as his Boston,
   Only as gentle and frightened
     As the little town he clings to.

Man does not live in the giant city
   Its arms are too big to hold him,
   Its voice too loud to hear him.
   His tears are just as lonely in San Francisco
       As in Fresno.
   The nights can be as empty, the days as dark
   As many lonely people shuffling through the park
   Till man finds his street, his tree
   His patch of sun or snow or gentle grass
   His place to rest, his chair, his ancient Mass
   Or just a thirsty plant that asks for water
   A pet or two, a son or daughter
   And memories, and hopes and dreams
   To know that at the end of every day
   Somewhere in his city is a town where he can stay.

WHO WILL MAKE
THE CITY JOYFUL?

Who will make the city joyful
　Who will wipe away its tears?
Who will fill the streets with gladness
　Who will calm the old folks' fears?
Who will tell the children stories
　Who will make their clear eyes gleam?
Who will keep the men from killing
　Who will give the women dreams?

Maybe twenty thousand minstrels
　Twenty thousand poets' words
Maybe fifty thousand dancers
　Maybe clowns and talking birds
Flowers on all the city's corners
　Trees on all the city streets
Maybe fragrance from the sewers
　Sing-alongs in subway seats.

Maybe buses painted purple
　Maybe no more numbered days
Bells that ring in all the buildings
　Merchants learning how to play
Maybe parks for picnic lunches
　Waterfalls and bubbling streams
　Maybe flowers on cold computers -
Crowning IBM machines.

Maybe plumbers playing trumpets
　　Salesmen strumming their guitars
Lawyers nursing tender flowers
　　Businessmen exploring stars
Maybe potters, weavers, artists
　　Craftsmen, architects who dare,
Maybe muralists and sculptors
　　Maybe anyone who cares.

Maybe honest politicians
　　Radicals with angry screams
Maybe socialists and Marxists
　　Maybe silent men who dream
Maybe shoppers loving beggars
　　Gently smiling flower maids
Those who listen to the children
　　Those who still enjoy parades.

Who will sit among the flowers
　　See the sun and sky above?
Who will make the city joyful
　　Who will make us laugh and love?
Maybe mothers loving babies
　　Maybe gentle eyes that see.
Or beyond the other maybes
　　Maybe you and maybe me.

SOMETIMES
I REALIZE

Sometimes I realize
  That there are bus drivers who like their jobs
  Black kids who are happy
  Women who enjoy being mothers
  Freeway snarls that give people time to think
  Policemen who can make mistakes and laugh
  Old folks who aren't despondent
  Factory workers who hum all day
  Married couples who are in love
  Girls who aren't afraid to walk at night
  Kids who think school is really fun.
Sometimes I realize
  That there are teachers who enjoy their classes
  Longshoremen who think they're well paid
  Hunters who don't have a masculine hangup
  Children who love their parents
  Rich people who could be poor with dignity
  Girls who don't want bigger breasts
  Men and women who aren't afraid to die
  Doctors who care and don't overcharge
  Politicians who tell the truth.
Sometimes I realize that I am very happy.

INFORMATION ABOUT BOOKS AND TAPES AND
APPEARANCES BY JAMES KAVANAUGH

The *Steven J. Nash Publishing Company* will supply you with all books and tapes of James Kavanaugh currently available. To receive information about James Kavanaugh's *new* books or tapes, lectures and workshops; to arrange appearances or TV and radio interviews; or for *The James Kavanaugh Newsletter,* write to:

STEVEN J. NASH PUBLISHING
P.O. Box 2115
Highland Park, Illinois 60035

or Call:
1-800-843-8545

QUALITY PAPERBACK BOOKS OF JAMES KAVANAUGH
by STEVEN J. NASH:

There Are Men Too Gentle To Live Among Wolves *(65th Printing)* In this moving classic, Kavanaugh writes: "I am one of the searchers. There are, I believe, millions of us. We searchers are ambitious only for life itself, for everything beautiful it can provide . . . Most of all we want to love and to be loved, to live in a relationship that will not impede our wandering, nor prevent our search, nor lock us in prison walls . . ."

Will You Be My Friend? *(56th Printing)* Kavanaugh writes in this powerful, poetic reflection on true friendship: "Friendship is freedom, is flowing, is rare. It does not need stimulation, it stimulates itself. It trusts, understands, grows, explores, it smiles and weeps. It does not exhaust or cling, expect or demand. It is—and that is enough—and it dreams a lot!"

Laughing Down Lonely Canyons *(1986)* Kavanaugh brings his special blend of compassion, insight, and gentle humor to life's hard and hurting times . . . to those periods in our lives when we finally confront loneliness and fear . . . "This is a book for the barely brave like me, who refuse to abandon their dream . . . It is for those who want to make of life the joy it was meant to be, who refuse to give up no matter the pain . . ."

From Loneliness To Love *(1988)* At a time when the past freedoms grow dim, it seems hard to make intimate connections. There's a new kind of sexual warfare in which everyone loses the healing power of love. Kavanaugh writes: "To move from loneliness to love means to take a risk . . . to create the kind of personal environment and support we need. This is a book of hope and reassurance that love is available and loneliness can end."

Search: A Guide For Those Who Dare Ask of Life Everything Good and Beautiful. *(Prose, 1989)* "**Search** provides 12 proven principles to move from self doubt through self awareness to self love. It is a celebration of one's creativity and unique beauty, rising from practical psychology to the spiritual power of our Inner Being in a journey to wholeness." James Kavanaugh frequently offers an exciting workshop based on this book in various parts of the country.

Today I Wondered About Love *(formerly Will You Still Love Me)* This book was written in San Francisco and captured the soul of that city. Burt Bacharach called this his "favorite Kavanaugh book."

Maybe If I Loved You More These passionate, lyrical poems confront forces that numb our senses and corrupt our values. Kavanaugh once again challenges us to be fully human, to move past private fears to simplicity and joy: "So much of life is spent trying to prove something...Maybe if I loved you more, I wouldn't have to prove anything!"

Sunshine Days and Foggy Nights This work contains Kavanaugh's most tender love poems, like the wondrous *Fragile Woman:* "to tender for sex, who will surely die—if tonight I do not love you." In words reminiscent of Joseph Campbell, he tells of the energy of any creative life: "The work I find most significant drains the least energy...my distractions are usually more creative than my resolutions."

Winter Has Lasted Too Long Kavanaugh sings of personal freedom and real love in a superb preface: "We shall be as free as we want, as mad as we are, as honest as we can. We shall accept no price for our integrity...This book is a heart's recognition that truth matters, love is attainable, and spring will begin tomorrow." Herein is the famed, "How much love I wasted on those I never loved."

Walk Easy On The Earth The book was inspired by three years Kavanaugh spent immersed in nature in a remote cabin in the California gold country. "I do not focus on the world's despair," he writes. "I am forever renewed by spring splashing over granite rocks, or a cautious deer emerging into twilight. I know then that I will survive all my personal fears and realize my finest dreams."

A Fable: The Story of Love and Greed A powerful, eloquent prose tale that touches the deepest chords in the human struggle of lust and love, passion and peace. Dear Abby says: "It is a powerful tale of our times. A classic! I loved it!" The Detroit Free Press says: "Kavanaugh spins a sentence until it sings."

Celebrate the Sun: A Love Story A moving prose allegory about the life of Harry Langendorf Pelican, dedicated to "those who take time to celebrate the sun—and are grateful!" Alan Watts called it: "A stirring and unforgettable story that unites wondrously the wisdom of East and West."

The Crooked Angel James Kavanaugh's only children's story, newly illustrated in four colors, tells of two angels "with crooked little wings" who escape from isolation and sadness through friendship and laughter. A particular Christmas delight that sold out wherever it was displayed.

The Tears and Laughter Of A Man's Soul *(1990 Hardback)* "His most mature and personal ever!"—LA TIMES. With the power that has won "thousands of readers who never liked poetry before."—SAN FRAN. CHRONICLE. Kavanaugh touches our hearts, gently leading us from anxiety beyond dogmas, leading to the profound experience of "the Power within." He makes us laugh aloud and weeps with us in our struggle for freedom and peace. He writes as a man "whose theories have been tested in the laboratory of vast experience"—TAMPA TRIBUNE. The man who 20 years ago challenged religions and culture itself, emerges as a brave explorer whose struggles reflect the joy and hope of the human spirit. This is no book of poetic rhetoric, but "a saga of life and near death, scars and victory, falling and forever rising! It is the *tears and laughter of a man's soul!*"